Bible
Teachings
made
easy

Mark Water

Bible Teachings Made Easy
Hendrickson Publishers, Inc.
P.O. Box 3473
Peabody, Massachusetts 01961-3473

Original edition published in
English under the title *"Bible
Teachings Made Easy"* by Hunt
& Thorpe, Alresford, Hants, UK.

Designed and produced
by Tony Cantale Graphics

First printing — September 1998

Printed in Hong Kong / China

Photography supplied by John
Foxx, Goodshoot, Digital Vision
and Tony Cantale

Illustrations by
Tony Cantale Graphics

Contents

Special pull-out chart
A bird's-eye view of Bible teaching themes

What does the Bible teach about itself?

A key verse

The Bible is a very practical book. It guides us on what we should *believe* and how we should *behave*.

> "All Scripture is God-breathed and is useful for teaching, rebuking, correcting and training in righteousness, so that the man of God may be thoroughly equipped for every good work." *2 Timothy 3:16*

The Bible is a book about God

The Bible is a book all about God. It reveals to human beings who God is and how he wants us to live. As the psalmist put it,

> "The LORD has made his salvation known
> and revealed his righteousness to the nations."
> *Psalm 98:2*

The Bible is a book about salvation

• The Bible shows God's rescue plan for delivering us from our sins.

> "The Scriptures ... are able to make you wise for salvation through faith in Christ Jesus." *2 Timothy 3:15*

• God is the Savior.

> "You are God my Savior." *Psalm 25:5*

• Jesus is the Savior.

> "The Father has sent his Son to be the Savior of the world." *1 John 4:14*

• Jesus came to save.

> "The Son of Man came to seek and to save what was lost." *Luke 19:10*

The Bible is a book about having faith in God

The Bible provides the foundation for our faith in Jesus, as it records what Jesus said and did.

"Faith comes from hearing the message, and the message is heard through the word of Christ." *Romans 10:17*

The law of the LORD

Psalm 19 tells us the purpose of the Bible (the law of the LORD).

"The law of the LORD is perfect,
  reviving the soul.
The statutes of the LORD are
    trustworthy,
  making wise the simple.
The precepts of the LORD are
    right,
  giving joy to the heart.
The commands of the LORD are
    radiant,
  giving light to the eyes."
Psalm 19:7-8

Did God really make the world in seven days?

Explaining creation

The creation of the world is described in the Book of Genesis in terms which made sense to readers in early times. It does not attempt to answer the question of how the world was made. Modern science does attempt to answer that question.

Genesis

The word "Genesis" means "beginning" or "origins." The title of the Book of Genesis in Hebrew, *Bere'shit*, is taken from Genesis 1:1, "In the beginning."

The Bible teaches that God was active before the creation of our world. Paul said that God "chose us in him before the creation of the world to be holy and blameless in his sight." *Ephesians 1:4*

God is assumed

The Bible never tries to prove the existence of God. It just describes those who do not believe in him as fools: "The fool says in his heart, "There is no God."" *Psalm 14:1*

Genesis does not attempt to prove that God made the world, it just states that he did: "In the beginning God created the heavens and the earth." *Genesis 1:1*

God is everywhere in Genesis

In the beginning
God created...	*Genesis 1:1*
... God said...	*Genesis 1:3*
... God saw...	*Genesis 1:4*
... God made...	*Genesis 1:7*
... God called...	*Genesis 1:10*
... God blessed...	*Genesis 1:28*
... God finished...	*Genesis 2:2*

Science versus the Bible

Emerging scientific theories do not threaten the validity of the Book of Genesis. Science itself is in a constant state of change and development. For example, Professor Stephen Hawking of Cambridge University in England frequently challenges widely held theories about the big bang (how the world began), the big crunch (how it will end), black holes and parallel universes.

While science tackles the question of how the world began, the Bible answers the questions of who created the world and why. There is no conflict between science and the Bible.

God is the creator

The Bible teaches that God is the creator of the world. Melchizedek said to Abram (Abraham), "Blessed be Abram by God Most High, Creator of heaven and earth." *Genesis 14:19*

We are not here by chance. The world did not come into existence as a result of a random combinination of certain atoms. God created it.

Was the world made in seven days?

Genesis chapter one talks about seven days when the world was created: "God said, "Let there be light," ... and there was evening, and there was morning – the first day." *Genesis 1:3, 5*

The Hebrew word for "day" (*yom*) can mean a period of twenty-four hours, but it can also mean a longer period of time. The Hebrew of Genesis 2:4 says, "This is the account of the heavens and the earth when they were created." In this example, the whole creative act is described as taking place in one "day."

Some Christians consider that theistic evolution is compatible with God's creation of the world. Others feel that the whole idea of evolution undermines the idea of God's special creation.

If God is so powerful, why does evil seem to win?

The nature of God

It is wrong to blame God for all the evil in the world. When evil seems to submerge the world, we must remember who God is.

God is against evil and against evil people

• Some of Jesus' sternest words were directed against evil people.

"Whoever welcomes a little child like this in my name welcomes me. But if anyone causes one of these little ones who believes in me to sin, it would be better for him to have a large millstone hung around his neck and to be drowned in the depths of the sea." *Matthew 18:5-6*

Jesus fought against evil

• Jesus spent his life fighting the manifestations of evil which came into his path.

"When evening came, many who were demon-possessed were brought to him, and he drove out the spirits with a word and healed all the sick. This was to fulfill what was spoken through the prophet Isaiah: 'He took up our infirmities and carried our diseases.'" *Matthew 8:16-17*

Jesus defeated evil on the cross

• "And having disarmed the powers and authorities, [Jesus] made a public spectacle of them, triumphing over them by the cross." *Colossians 2:15*

The picture here is of a soldier stripped not only of his armor, but of his clothes, so complete was his defeat. It symbolizes the total capitulation of a soldier.

• "The reason the Son of God appeared was to destroy the devil's work." *1 John 3:8*

Spiritual conflict

In so many places we see that the world is in Satan's grip: "The whole world is under the control of the evil one." *1 John 5:19*

Behind all evil, whenever it happened, is a spiritual conflict. There is a constant fight going on between good and evil: "Our struggle is ... against ... the spiritual forces of evil." *Ephesians 6:12*

Satan continues to do his best to lead us astray

"And there was war in heaven. Michael and his angels fought against the dragon, and the dragon and his angels fought back. But he was not strong enough, and they lost their place in heaven. The great dragon was hurled down – that ancient serpent called the devil, or Satan, who leads the whole world astray. He was hurled to the earth, and his angels with him." *Revelation 12:7-9*
This explains why there is so much evil in the world: Satan is at work.

Satan's days are numbered

"Then I heard a loud voice in heaven say:
'Now have come the salvation
    and the power and the
    kingdom of God,
    and the authority of his
    Christ.
For the accuser of our brothers,
    who accuses them before our
    God day and night,
    has been hurled down.
They overcame him
    by the blood of the Lamb
    and by the word of their
    testimony;
they did not love their lives so
    much
    as to shrink from death.
    ... he knows that his time is
    short.'"
Revelation 12:10-12

A final word from Jesus

"In this world you will have trouble. But take heart! I have overcome the world." *John 16:33*

What is the unforgivable sin?
Have I committed it?

Suggestions

Many people are really worried that they may have committed the unforgivable sin – be it murder, masturbation, swearing against God, or doing the most evil things imaginable. All these ideas are totally wrong.

What Jesus actually said

"Every sin and blasphemy will be forgiven men, but the blasphemy against the Spirit will not be forgiven. Anyone who speaks a word against the Son of Man will be forgiven, but anyone who speaks against the Holy Spirit will not be forgiven, either in this age or in the age to come."
Matthew 12:31-32

Who was Jesus talking to?

What provoked Jesus to say such a strange and serious thing? Let's look at the context of these words.

"Then they brought [to Jesus] a demon-possessed man who was blind and mute, and Jesus healed him, so that he could both talk and see. All the people were astonished and said, 'Could this be the Son of David?' But when the Pharisees heard this, they said, 'It is only by Beelzebub, the prince of demons, that this fellow drives out demons.'"
Matthew 12:22-24

No forgiveness

To say that Satan performed Jesus' miracles is unforgivable. Jesus said in Mark 3:29,

"Whoever blasphemes against the Holy Spirit will never be forgiven; he is guilty of an eternal sin."

Jesus is not saying that there is any one sin which is so terrible that it cannot be forgiven, but that if a person is so warped as to regard good as evil, and evil as good, then he does not want to be forgiven, and cannot be forgiven. A person who does not want forgiveness can never be forgiven. "Blaspheme" here does not mean some kind of bad language or swearing, but relentless hostility to God.

Unbelievers

Some have theorized that the one sin that is unforgivable is the sin of "unbelief." That is to say that "unbelief" is the one sin that the blood of Jesus could not cover. Every other sin in the world can be forgiven, but if one fails to place one's faith in Jesus Christ and decides to remain in "unbelief" – then that sin of unbelief is not forgivable. It is a direct rebuff of the work of the Holy Spirit on one's heart.

Are you worried?

Anyone who is genuinely concerned that he may have committed the unforgivable sin, has not done so. For such a person will ask God for his forgiveness. It is only the person who does not think that he or she ever needs God's forgiveness, who may have committed this sin.

No one is turned away

Jesus said, "Whoever comes to me I will never drive away." *John 6:37*

Should Christians believe in angels?

Messengers

The word "angel," in Greek *angelos*, means "messenger."

Perhaps the most helpful definition of the ministry of angels appears in Hebrews 1:14, "Are not all angels ministering spirits sent to serve those who will inherit salvation?" From this verse we can deduce that angels:

- Are sent by God.
- Their work is to serve Christians.
- Are "spirits" in form, rather than human.

Angels serving God

Angels are always on hand to serve God and carry out his orders. They are linked with some of the most important of God's actions:

At the creation	"All the angels shouted for joy." *Job 38:7*
In the Garden of Eden	A "cherubim [was placed] to guard the way to the tree of life." *Genesis 3:24*
In the giving of the law	"The law was put into effect through angels." *Acts 7:53*
At the final judgment	"When the Son of Man comes in his glory, and all the angels with him, he will sit on his throne in heavenly glory." *Matthew 25:31*

Angels serving humans

Angels act as God's agents for the benefit of humankind.

People helped by angels	Bible quotation
Hagar After Sarah ill-treated her	"The angel of the LORD found Hagar near a spring. ... [He told her,] 'I will so increase your descendants that they will be too numerous to count.'" *Genesis 16:7, 10*
Elijah After his ordeal on Mount Carmel	"Elijah came to a broom tree, sat down under it and prayed that he might die. ... All at once an angel touched him and said, 'Get up and eat.'" *1 Kings 19:4-5*

Joseph Warning to escape to Egypt	"An angel of the Lord appeared to Joseph in a dream. 'Get up,' he said, 'take the child and his mother and escape to Egypt.'" *Matthew 2:13*
Peter Escape from prison	"The night before Herod was to bring him to trial, Peter was sleeping between two soldiers, bound in two chains, and sentries stood guard at the entrance. Suddenly an angel of the Lord appeared and a light shone in the cell. He struck Peter on the side and woke him up. 'Quick, get up!' he said, and the chains fell off Peter's wrists." *Acts 12:6-7*
Paul Just before a shipwreck	"Last night an angel of the God whose I am and whom I serve stood beside me and said, 'Do not be afraid, Paul. You must stand trial before Caesar; and God has graciously given you the lives of all who sail with you.'" *Acts 27:23-26*

Angels and Jesus

Angels looked after Jesus during his earthly life with special care and concern:

At Jesus' birth	"An angel of the Lord appeared to [shepherds]." *Luke 2:9*
After Jesus' temptations	"Angels came and attended [Jesus]." *Matthew 4:11*
During his time of agony in the Garden of Gethsemane	"An angel from heaven appeared to [Jesus] and strengthened him." *Luke 22:43*
At Jesus' resurrection	"There was a violent earthquake, for an angel of the Lord came down from heaven and, going to the tomb, rolled back the stone and sat on it." *Matthew 28:2*

Angels in disguise

"Do not forget to entertain strangers, for by so doing some people have entertained angels without knowing it." *Hebrews 13:2*

Is the Bible anti-women?

Jesus

The disciples were amazed when they found Jesus talking to a Samaritan woman one day. In those times, a rabbi would not talk to a woman in public. See John 4:27.

Women in Luke's Gospel

One of the striking things about Luke's Gospel is Jesus' attitude toward women, which was so different from the traditional Jewish one.

Respect for womanhood

The stories of the pregnancies of Elizabeth and Mary take up nearly all of the first eighty verses of Luke's Gospel.

The widow of Nain

Luke is the only gospel writer to include this story. Jesus brought back to life "a dead person... – the only son of his mother, and she was a widow." *Luke 7:12*

Women cared for Jesus

"After this, Jesus traveled about from one town and village to another, proclaiming the good news of the kingdom of God. The Twelve were with him, and also some women who had been cured of evil spirits and diseases: Mary (called Magdalene) from whom seven demons had come out; Joanna the wife of Chuza, the manager of Herod's household; Susanna; and many others. These women were helping to support them out of their own means." *Luke 8:1-3*

Women were faithful to the end

"But all those who knew him, including the women who had followed him from Galilee, stood at a distance watching these things. ... The women who had come with Jesus from Galilee followed Joseph and saw the tomb and how his body was laid in it." *Luke 23:49, 55*

Women were the first people to discover Jesus' resurrection

"On the first day of the week, very early in the morning, the women took the spices they had prepared and went to the tomb. They found the stone rolled away from the tomb, but when they entered, they did not find the body of the Lord Jesus." *Luke 24:1-3*

Women remained faithful to Jesus after his ascension

"They all joined together constantly in prayer, along with the women and Mary the mother of Jesus, and with his brothers." *Acts 1:14*

Prophetesses in the Bible

Miriam	*Exodus 15:20*
Deborah	*Judges 4:4*
Huldah	*2 Kings 22:14-20*
Anna	*Luke 2:36-38*
Philip's four daughters	*Acts 21:8-9*

The guiding principle

The Bible leaves no room for male chauvinism or for treating women as second-class citizens: "There is neither Jew nor Greek, slave nor free, male nor female, for you are all one in Christ Jesus." *Galatians 3:28*

Does the Bible say anything about abortion and euthanasia?

God is our creator

The development of the unborn baby in the womb is the work of God:

"You alone created my inner being.
You knitted me together inside my mother."
Psalm 139:13 (GW)

"[Job asks] Did you not ... clothe me with skin and flesh and knit me together with bones and sinews?"
Job 10:10-11

"My bones were not hidden from you
when I was being made in secret,
when I was being skillfully woven in an underground workshop.
Your eyes saw me when I was only a fetus."
Psalm 139:15-16 (GW)

"I will give thanks to you
because I have been so amazingly and miraculously made.
Your works are miraculous,
and my soul is fully aware of this."
Psalm 139:14 (GW)

The psalmist emphasizes continuity

The psalmist is unaware of any discontinuity between being an embryo, a baby, a youth and an adult. He talks about himself as "I" and "me" in four states of being:

In his present state	"You know when I sit and when I rise." *Psalm 139:2*
In his past	"You have searched me." *Psalm 139:2*
In his future	"Your hand would guide me." *Psalm 139:10*
In his pre-born state	"You knitted me together inside my mother." *Psalm 139:13 (GW)*

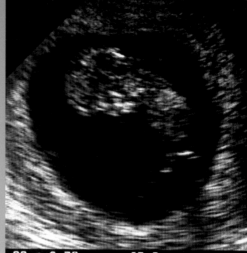

Good motives?

Some people are open to abortion in very defined circumstances – for example if the mother's life is in danger, or if the baby is severely handicapped. Others are against abortion in all circumstances.

What if a much-loved relative is in agony all day and all night from an incurable illness, what is the kind and loving thing to do? Some would say that if the person has given consent, he should be helped to die quickly with a fatal overdose.

But because life is a gift from God, can it ever be right to take another person's life? The Bible tells us: "My times are in your [God's] hands." *Psalm 31:15*

The Bible is on the side of the weak

As a general principle, the Bible comes down in favor of the weak. Nobody is weaker than an unborn baby, or someone in the final stages of a terminal illness.

"For [God] will deliver the needy who cry out, the afflicted who have no one to help. He will take pity on the weak and the needy and save the needy from death. He will rescue them from oppression and violence, for precious is their blood in his sight." *Psalm 72:12-14*

See also: *Where can I find Bible teaching on contemporary issues?*, page 28.

Can we really believe in Satan today?

Jesus believed in Satan

Jesus was the Son of God, so we accept all he taught. This includes his teaching about the devil.

Jesus was tempted by the devil, but said to him, "Away from me, Satan!" *Matthew 4:10*

Satan is still very busy

Satan tries to stop people from keeping God's word in their hearts:

"Those along the path are the ones who hear, and then the devil comes and takes away the word from their hearts, so that they may not believe and be saved." *Luke 8:12*

Paul and Peter

• Paul was attacked by Satan:

"To keep me from becoming conceited because of these surpassingly great revelations, there was given me a thorn in my flesh, a messenger of Satan, to torment me." *2 Corinthians 12:7*

• Peter warned that Satan was lurking:

"Your enemy the devil prowls around like a roaring lion looking for someone to devour. Resist him, standing firm in the faith, because you know that your brethren throughout the world are undergoing the same kind of sufferings." *1 Peter 5:8-9*

Satan and the spiritual battle

Christians are engaged in a spiritual battle all their lives.

"Put on the full armor of God so that you can take your stand against the devil's schemes. For our struggle is not against flesh and blood, but against the rulers, against the authorities, against the powers of this dark world and against the spiritual forces of evil in the heavenly realms." *Ephesians 6:11-12*

Jesus came to defeat Satan

"The reason the Son of God appeared was to destroy the devil's work." *1 John 3:8*

Some of Satan's characteristics

We are told to be on the lookout for the devil. It helps to know what he is like, so we can be on our guard.

• Satan is scheming

"... in order that Satan might not outwit us. For we are not unaware of his schemes."
2 Corinthians 2:11

• Satan tempts

"I was afraid that in some way the tempter might have tempted you and our efforts might have been useless." *1 Thessalonians 3:5*

• Satan deceives

"The coming of the lawless one will be in accordance with the work of Satan displayed in all kinds of counterfeit miracles, signs and wonders, and in every sort of evil that deceives those who are perishing."
2 Thessalonians 2:9-10

See also:
Possessed by the devil, or mental illness?, page 20.

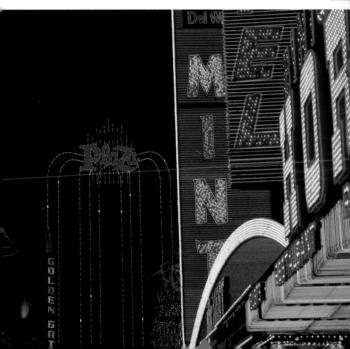

Possessed by the devil, or mental illness?

Satan is powerful

Satan is a defeated foe. But he is still very powerful:

"The whole world is under the control of the evil one." *1 John 5:19*

Satan "enters" into people:

"As soon as Judas took the bread, Satan entered into him." *John 13:27*

Jesus expelled many demons

"God anointed Jesus of Nazareth with the Holy Spirit and power, ... he went around doing good and healing all who were under the power of the devil, because God was with him." *Acts 10:38*

People Jesus helped

Two demon-possessed men who lived among the tombs.	*Matthew 8:28-34*
A demon-possessed man who could not talk.	*Matthew 9:32-33*
A demon-possessed man who was blind and mute.	*Matthew 12:22*
A demon-possessed daughter.	*Matthew 15:21-28*
A demon-possessed boy.	*Matthew 17:14-18*
A man possessed of an evil spirit in a synagogue.	*Mark 1:21-28*
Various people possessed by demons.	*Mark 1:32-34*
Mary, from whom seven demons had been expelled.	*Luke 8:2*

The demon-possessed boy

"When they came to the crowd, a man approached Jesus and knelt before him. 'Lord, have mercy on my son,' he said. 'He has seizures and is suffering greatly. He often falls into the fire or into the water. I brought him to your disciples, but they could not heal him.'

'O unbelieving and perverse generation,' Jesus replied, 'how long shall I stay with you?... Bring the boy here to me.' Jesus rebuked the demon, and it came out of the boy, and he was healed from that moment."
Matthew 17:14-18

Exorcism and mental illness

The writers of the gospels are careful to distinguish between all forms of illness, and possession by demons. However, sometimes sickness and possession occurred together.

"[Jesus] drove out the spirits with a word and healed all the sick." *Matthew 8:16*

"News about [Jesus] spread all over Syria, and people brought to him all who were ill with various diseases, those suffering from severe pain, the demon-possessed, those having seizures, and the paralysed, and he healed them." *Matthew 4:24*

The possessed

The gospel writers always emphasize that the actions and words of the demon-possessed come from evil spirits.

- **Actions of the possessed.**
  "Whenever the evil spirits saw [Jesus], they fell down before him and cried out." *Mark 3:11*
- **Words of the possessed.**
  "The demons begged Jesus ..." *Matthew 8:31*

Jesus treated possession as a reality

"[Jesus] appointed twelve – designating them apostles – that they might be with him and that he might send them out to preach and to have authority to drive out demons." *Mark 3:14-15*

See also:
Can we really believe in Satan today?,
page 18.

Is the Bible really against sex?

"No sex, thank you, we're Christians!"

Non-Christians might think that "No sex, thank you, we're Christians" is the attitude Christians have toward sex. A summary of the Bible teaching on the subject of sex looks very negative.

- No fornication. *See 1 Thessalonians 4:3.*
- No adultery. *See Exodus 20:14.*
- No sex between men and men. *See Romans 1:27.*
- No sex between women and women. *See Romans 1:26.*

God "invented" sex

God is the giver of all good things, including sex. The Bible teaches that God intended that the only sexual union should be between a wife and a husband.

"For this reason a man will leave his father and mother and be united to his wife, and they will become one flesh." *Genesis 2:24*

The Song of Solomon

Some Jews took the Book of Song of Songs, (the Song of Solomon) to be an allegory about God's love for Israel. Some Christians view it as an allegory about Jesus' love for his Church.

The Song of Solomon is also interpreted as a love poem which extols the virtue of love between a man and a woman. It contains a number of erotic verses and for this reason, it is said that rabbis were once forbidden to read it until they were thirty years old.

A guide for a good marriage

The Song of Solomon is a useful guide on how to have a healthy relationship in marriage. In many ways, it goes against the prevailing attitudes of today's society.

Love and its joy

"How delightful is your love, my
    sister, my bride!
  How much more pleasing is
    your love than wine,
  and the fragrance of your
    perfume than any spice!"
Song of Songs 4:10

"Let him kiss me with the kisses of
    his mouth –
  for your love is more delightful
    than wine."
Song of Songs 1:2

"How beautiful you are and how
    pleasing,
  O love, with your delights!"
Song of Songs 7:6

Do not treat love lightly

"Daughters of Jerusalem, I charge
    you:
  Do not arouse or awaken love
    until it so desires."
Song of Songs 8:4

Love and its strength

"Place me like a seal over your
    heart,
  like a seal on your arm;
for love is as strong as death."
Song of Songs 8:6

"Many waters cannot quench
    love;
  rivers cannot wash it away."
Song of Songs 8:7

Love and its value

"If one were to give
    all the wealth of his house for
    love,
  it would be utterly scorned."
Song of Songs 8:7

Commitment to love

"I belong to my lover."
Song of Songs 7:10

"My lover is mine and I am his."
Song of Songs 2:16

Respect for marriage

The writer of the Book of Hebrews says, "Marriage should be honored by all, and the marriage bed kept pure."
Hebrews 13:4

How can I live in the world but remain apart from its bad side?

God's world

It is true that we live in a polluted and evil world today. But when God made the world, "God saw all that he had made and it was very good." *Genesis 1:31*

Heaven is our real home

Jesus said, "In my Father's house are many rooms; if it were not so, I would have told you. I am going there to prepare a place for you. And if I go and prepare a place for you, I will come back and take you to be with me that you also may be where I am." *John 14:2-3*

Jesus was not a recluse

- Jesus attended the wedding party at Cana. *See John 2:1-11.*
- While Jesus cared greatly for the poor, he also accepted invitations to eat with wealthy people. He was even accused of being too partial to drink.

Jesus said, "For John [the Baptist] came neither eating nor drinking, and they say, 'He has a demon.' The Son of Man came eating and drinking, and they say, 'Here is a glutton and a drunkard, a friend of tax collectors and sinners.' But wisdom is proved right by her actions." *Matthew 11:18-19*

Dangers and characteristics of the world

- **The world is in the grip of the enemy**

  "The whole world is under the control of the evil one." *1 John 5:19*

- **Worldly temptations try to entice us.**

  "Don't let the world around you squeeze you into its own mold, but let God re-mold your minds from within, so that you may prove in practice that the plan of God for you is good, meets all his demands and moves towards the goal of true maturity." *Romans 12:2, J.B. Phillips' translation*

- **Worldly delights will not last**

  "The world and its desires pass away, but the person who does the will of God lives for ever." *1 John 2:17*

- **The world is being led astray**

  "The devil ... Satan ... leads the whole world astray." *Revelation 12:9*

How to enjoy God's world

- **Remember who provides us with things to enjoy**

  "God ... richly provides us with everything for our enjoyment." *1 Timothy 6:17*

- **Receive these things with a prayer of thanks to God**

  "[False teachers] forbid people to marry and order them to abstain from certain foods, which God created to be received with thanksgiving by those who believe and who know the truth. For everything God created is good, and nothing is to be rejected if it is received with thanksgiving, because it is consecrated by the word of God and prayer." *1 Timothy 4:3-5*

Light for the world

Jesus did not want the world to influence Christians, but he told Christians to influence the world.

Jesus said, "You are the light of the world. A city on a hill cannot be hidden. Neither do people light a lamp and put it under a bowl. Instead they put it on its stand, and it gives light to everyone in the house. In the same way, let your light shine before men, that they may see your good deeds and praise your Father in heaven." *Matthew 5:14-16*

Is God like a loving parent?

Abba

Abba is the Aramaic word for "Father." The word is not as formal as "Father" and has been translated as "Daddy." Jesus used this word when he prayed:

> "'*Abba*, Father,' he said, 'everything is possible for you. Take this cup from me. Yet not what I will, but what you will.'"
> *Mark 14:36*

Christians are also to use the word *Abba* in their prayers.

> "Because you are sons, God sent his Spirit of his Son into our hearts, the Spirit who calls out, '*Abba*, Father.'" *Galatians 4:6*

God is called "Father" by the Old Testament spokesmen

God cared for the people of Israel, as a father cares for his children.

- So says Moses: "Is he not your Father, your Creator, who made you and formed you?" *Deuteronomy 32:6*
- So says Isaiah: "But you are our Father, ... you, O LORD, are our Father, our Redeemer from of old is your name." *Isaiah 63:16*

- So says Jeremiah: "I will lead them beside streams of water on a level path where they will not stumble, because I am Israel's father." *Jeremiah 31:9*

Jesus talks about the "Father"

Jesus told people that God would care for them as a parent, providing what they needed, so they had no need to worry:

> "And why do you worry about your clothes? See how the lilies of the field grow. They do not labor or spin. Yet I tell you that not even Solomon in all his splendor was dressed like one of these. If this is how God clothes the grass of the field, which is here today and tomorrow is thrown into the fire, will he not much more clothe you, O you of little faith?
>
> So do not worry, saying, 'What shall we eat?' or 'What shall we drink?' or 'What shall we wear?' For the pagans run after all these things, and your heavenly Father knows that you need them."
> *Matthew 7:28-32*

God disciplines us for our own good

Nobody enjoys being disciplined. But the writer of the Book of Hebrews reminds us that God disciplines us, his children, as a parent might.

When we are corrected by God it may seem a tough experience. But the following quotation from Hebrews points out three positive aspects of God's discipline.

- It is a word of encouragement.
- We should not lose heart when disciplined.
- It is those the Lord loves who are disciplined.

"And you have forgotten that word of encouragement that addresses you as sons:
'My son, do not make light of the Lord's discipline,
  and do not lose heart when he rebukes you,
because the Lord disciplines those he loves,
  and he punishes everyone he accepts as a son.'"
Hebrews 12:5-6

God has "mothering" characteristics

The prophet Isaiah paints a picture of God as a mother who will never forget her child, and as a mother bringing comfort to a distressed child.

"Can a mother forget the baby at her breast
and have no compassion on the child she has borne?
Though she may forget,
I will not forget you"
Isaiah 49:15

"As a mother comforts her child, so will I comfort you."
Isaiah 66:13

27

Where can I find Bible teaching on contemporary issues?

Principles

A number of our modern ethical problems, such as cloning, did not exist in Bible times. However, there are certain *principles* laid down in the Bible which shed light on the moral problems we face today. Much of Jesus' teaching in the Sermon on the Mount, Matthew 5–7, gives straightforward guidance on subjects such as adultery, divorce, and revenge.

Specific Issues

Caring for others

"Religion that God our Father accepts as pure and faultless is this: to look after orphans and widows in their distress and to keep oneself from being polluted by the world." *James 1:27*

Justice

Our community should be a caring one, and one in which justice is upheld.

"He upholds the cause of the oppressed
and gives food to the hungry.
The LORD sets prisoners free,
and the LORD gives sight to the blind,
the LORD lifts up those who are bowed down,
the LORD loves the righteous.
The LORD watches over the alien and sustains the fatherless and the widow,
but he frustrates the way of the wicked."
Psalm 146:7-9

The poor should be looked after

"This is what the LORD says:
'For three sins of Israel,
even for four, I will not turn back my wrath.
They sell the righteous for silver,
and the needy for a pair of sandals.
They trample on the heads of the poor
as upon the dust of the ground
and deny justice to the oppressed.'"
Amos 2:6-7

Christians should be involved in social action

"If anyone has material possessions and sees his brother in need but has no pity on him, how can the love of God be in him?" *1 John 3:17*
"Let us not become weary in doing good ... Therefore, as we have opportunity, let us do good to all people, especially to those who belong to the family of believers." *Galatians 6:9a, 10*

Remember the nature of God

We should think and behave in ways which are in line with who God is: "the compassionate and gracious God, slow to anger, abounding in love and faithfulness." *Exodus 34:6*

Look in the letters

Nearly all the letters in the New Testament are divided into two major parts. The first part is usually doctrinal, with instructions about what to believe, and the second part is usually ethical, with guidelines on how to behave. These ethical instructions, given for Christians living in the first century, contain principles which can guide us today.

Theme	Letter
Christians and the State	*Romans 13:1-7*
Immorality in the Church	*1 Corinthians 5*
Taking a fellow Christian to court	*1 Corinthians 6*
Questions about marriage and divorce	*1 Corinthians 7*
Christians and money	*2 Corinthians 8*
Christian unity	*Ephesians 4*
Sexual morality	*1 Thessalonians 4:1-8*
The way we live	*1 Thessalonians 4:11-12*
Idleness	*2 Thessalonians 3:6-15*
Slavery	*Philemon*
Qualifications of a Christian leader	*1 Timothy 3*

See also:
Does the Bible really favor the poor?, page 32.
Is the Bible anti-women?, page 14.
Is the Bible really against sex?, page 22.
Does the Bible have anything to say about abortion and euthanasia?, page 16.

Where can I find comfort in the Bible?

The God of all comfort

Knowing where to find words of comfort in the Bible can be a boon for us as well as for when we want to help others.

> "Praise be to the God and Father of our Lord Jesus Christ, the Father of compassion and the God of all comfort, who comforts us in all our troubles, so that we can comfort those in any trouble with the comfort we ourselves have received from God."
> *2 Corinthians 1:3-4*

Dipping into the psalms

Many of the psalms are about God and his comfort. It is sometimes better to concentrate on God than on our own troubles.

God in the psalms

• God and his power	*Psalm 26*
• God and his love	*Psalm 136*
• God and his glory	*Psalm 48*
• God and his creation	*Psalm 8*
• God and his forgiveness	*Psalm 32*
• God and his suffering	*Psalm 22*
• God and his greatness	*Psalm 145*
• God and his goodness	*Psalm 34*

God and his goodness

"I will extol the LORD at all times;
  his praise will always be on my
    lips.
My soul will boast in the LORD;
  let the afflicted hear and rejoice.
Glorify the LORD with me:
  let us exalt his name together.
I sought the LORD, and he
    answered me;
  he delivered me from all my
    fears.
Those who look to him are
    radiant;
  their faces are never covered
    with shame.
This poor man called, and the
    LORD heard him;
  he saved him out of all his
    troubles.
The angel of the LORD encamps
    around those who fear him,
  and he delivers them."
Psalm 34:1-7

Psalms for different needs
- When you are broken-hearted   *Psalm 147*
- When you are lonely   *Psalm 25*
- When you need God's guidance   *Psalm 37*
- When you need God's care   *Psalm 23*
- When you are depressed   *Psalm 42*
- When you need God's pardon   *Psalm 130*
- When you are building a home   *Psalm 127*
- When you are sad   *Psalm 6*
- When you have sinned   *Psalm 51*
- When you are upset   *Psalm 109*

God's comfort is found ...
- For those who mourn   *Isaiah 61:2*
- God's promise of comfort   *Isaiah 66:13*
- Comfort and joy linked   *Jeremiah 31:13*

God's comfort comes through people
- You should comfort and forgive others   *2 Corinthians 2:7*
- How the apostle Paul was comforted   *Colossians 4:11*
- Prophecy brings comfort   *1 Corinthians 14:3*

Does the Bible really favor the poor?

The poor man's cloak

A number of the laws in the Old Testament were aimed at the needs of the poor, such as the following one, which recognized that the only way a poor person could keep warm at night was by wrapping himself up in his cloak.

"If you take your neighbor's cloak as a pledge, return it to him by sunset, because his cloak is the only covering he has for his body. What else will he sleep in? When he cries out to me, I will hear, for I am compassionate." *Exodus 22:26-27*

Injustice

Underhand trading practices made life even harder for the poor. People were cheated by the use of false weights in the marketplace. God's spokesmen often condemned this practice in the Old Testament.

- "Use honest scales and honest weights." *Leviticus 19:36*
- "Do not have two differing weights." *Deuteronomy 25:13*
- "Accurate weights are [God's] delight." *Proverbs 11:1*

Jesus and the poor

Jesus had many things to say about how people should treat the poor.

- "Sell your possessions and give to the poor." *Luke 12:33*
- Jesus said to his host, "When you give a luncheon or dinner, do not invite your friends, your brothers or relatives, or your rich neighbors; if you do, they may invite you back and so you will be repaid. But when you give a banquet, invite the poor, the crippled, the lame, the blind, and you will be blessed. Although they cannot repay you, you will be repaid at the resurrection of the righteous." *Luke 14:12-14*

Sheep and goats

Jesus expected his followers to care for the poor, the disadvantaged and the weak. He told the following story about the Day of Judgment at the end of the world.

"When the Son of Man comes in his glory, and all the angels with him, he will sit on his throne in heavenly glory. All the nations will be gathered before him, and he will separate the people one from another as a shepherd separates the sheep from the goats. He will put the sheep on his right and the goats on his left.

[Message to the sheep]
Then the King will say to those on his right, 'Come, you who are blessed by my Father, take your inheritance, the kingdom prepared for you since the creation of the world. For I was hungry and you gave me something to eat, I was thirsty and you gave me something to drink, I was a stranger and you invited me in, I needed clothes and you clothed me, I was sick and you looked after me, I was in prison and you came to visit me.'

Then the righteous will answer him, 'Lord, when did we see you hungry and feed you, or thirsty and give you something to drink? When did we see you a stranger and invite you in, or needing clothes and clothe you? When did we see you sick or in prison and go to visit you?'

The King will reply, 'I tell you the truth, whatever you did for one of the least of these brothers of mine, you did for me.'

[Message to the goats]
Then he will say to those on his left, 'Depart from me you who are cursed, into eternal fire prepared for the devil and his angels. For I was hungry and you gave me nothing to eat, I was thirsty and you gave me nothing to drink, I was a stranger and you did not invite me in, I needed clothes and you did not clothe me, I was sick and in prison and you did not look after me.'

They also will answer, 'Lord, when did we see you hungry or thirsty or a stranger or needing clothes or sick or in prison, and did not help you?'

He will reply, 'I tell you the truth, whatever you did not do for one of the least of these, you did not do for me.'

Then they will go away to eternal punishment, but the righteous to eternal life."
Matthew 25:31-46

What does the Bible say about race relations?

Martin Luther King Jr.

"I have a dream that my four children will one day live in a nation where they will not be judged by the color of their skin but by the content of their character."

This extract from one of the most famous speeches of all time was given by the Southern Baptist preacher, the Revd. Martin Luther King Jr., on the steps at the Lincoln Memorial in Washington D.C. on August 28, 1963.

Jesus said that God's love goes out to everyone:

"Your Father in heaven ... causes his sun to rise on the evil and the good, and sends rain on the righteous and the unrighteous." *Matthew 5:45*

Paul

Paul wrote in the first century that Christians should hold no prejudices on account of race, social standing or gender:

"There is neither Jew nor Greek, slave nor free, male nor female, for you are all one in Christ Jesus." *Galatians 3:28*

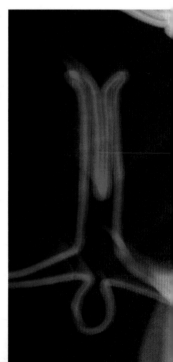

Jesus

In the Palestine of Jesus' time, there was a great deal of racial prejudice. The Samaritans, a people of mixed race, were regarded as foreigners, impure and "sinners." Also, attitudes to women were very different from those of today. Jesus made a point of demonstrating how bigoted people were.

• He made a despised Samaritan the hero of one of his most famous parables. *Read Luke 10:25-37.*
• Jewish teachers never lowered themselves to talking to women in public. When the disciples found Jesus talking to a woman, who was also a Samaritan, they were most suprised. *See John 4:1-42.*

Heaven

The picture John paints of heaven in the Book of Revelation reveals that all races will be welcomed there:

"After this I looked and there before me was a great multitude that no one could count, from every nation, tribe, people and language, standing before the throne and in front of the Lamb." *Revelation 7:9*

Does the Bible speak about the New Age movement and reincarnation?

The New Age movement

The New Age movement is an unstructured belief in "self" – a network of secular humanistic ideas and philosophies. It is a search to tap into the universal "force" or "energy." There is no specific leader. The New Age movement wants to bring about change: change in politics, change in religion, change in health practices. These changes, followers believe, will usher in a New Age that will be characterized by world harmony.

So what's wrong with the New Age movement?

Many of the hopes of the New Age movement are shared by all people of goodwill, including Christians. But there are a number of New Age practices and beliefs which the Bible condemns outright:

- Occult practices.
- Do-it-yourself morality.
- Belief that God is in everything (pantheism).
- Mystical meditation, sometimes assisted by drugs.

What does the Bible say?

The most dangerous aspect of the New Age movement is that it claims to offer spiritual reality. Many followers are lulled into believing that the New Age way can give them complete fulfillment. But what it claims to bring is nothing less than a spiritual counterfeit.

There are numerous Bible passages which specifically warn us not to be taken in by counterfeits:

- Counterfeit miracles
  Exodus 7:8-13
- Counterfeit converts
  2 Corinthians 11:26; 1 John 2:19
- Counterfeit Christs
  Matthew 24:5; Acts 5:36-37
- Counterfeit godliness
  2 Timothy 3:5
- Counterfeit prophets
  Matthew 7:15
- Counterfeit teaching
  1 Timothy 4:1-3

Jesus warns against counterfeit good deeds

"Watch out for false prophets. They come to you in sheep's clothing, but inwardly they are ferocious wolves. ... Many will say to me on that day, 'Lord, Lord, did we not prophesy in your name, and in your name drive out demons and perform many miracles?' Then I will tell them plainly, 'I never knew you. Away from me, you evil-doers!' "
Matthew 7:15, 22-23

If people do not believe in Jesus, they are likely to believe in anything!

Reincarnation

Reincarnation is defined as a new birth, or a second birth. It is belief in the rebirth of a soul in another body. In popular thinking, if you believe in reincarnation, in your next life you may return as an animal, or as some powerful ruler, depending on how good a life you have led in this present life.

Reincarnation or resurrection?
New Age followers sometimes confuse reincarnation with resurrection.

While the Bible gives no grounds at all for believing in reincarnation, it has a great deal of evidence for the resurrection of Jesus. The key Bible chapters on Jesus' resurrection are *Matthew 28; Mark 16; Luke 24; John 20; 1 Corinthians 15.*

Reincarnation and judgment
One thing that the New Age movement does *not* teach is that we each have to face being judged by God after we die. After death there is no reincarnation, but there is judgment.

The key Bible verse on judgment says, "...Man is destined to die once, and after that to face judgment."
Hebrews 9:27
This verse is opposed to the idea of reincarnation. It teaches that we die *once*.

Who spoke most about judgment in the Bible?

Jesus – "meek and mild"?

Jesus was the most compassionate and caring person who has ever lived. But the impression the often-used phrase "gentle Jesus meek and mild" gives (a phrase which is *not* found in the Bible) is misleading.

Nobody in the Old Testament or in the New Testament spoke more about God's judgment than Jesus did. In John 9:39, he said that he had come into the world to give judgment.

Jesus and judgment

- Jesus stated that judgment hinges on acceptance or rejection of him.
- Jesus explained that a judgment of "eternal life" or "condemnation" happens in this life.
- Jesus revealed that he is the judge.

"I tell you the truth, whoever hears my word and believes him who sent me has eternal life and will not be condemned; he has crossed over from death to life. ... [The Father] has given [the Son] authority to judge because he is the Son of Man." *John 5:24, 26*

Jesus takes us to heaven

Jesus came to earth so that we might go to heaven:

"For God did not send his Son into the world to condemn the world, but to save the world through him." *John 3:17*

"God ... wants all people to be saved and to come to a knowledge of the truth." *1 Timothy 2:4*

Jesus' last recorded words to anyone outside his close followers and family were,

"Today you will be with me in paradise." *Luke 23:43*

The word for hell

When Jesus talked about hell, he described an actual place people all knew about – the Valley of Hinnom. It was a rubbish dump, just outside Jerusalem, where all the city's rubbish was thrown, and where it was often burned. The Jews pictured this place as the place of punishment for the wicked. Jesus spoke in Aramaic and would have used the word *Gehinnam* for the Valley of Hinnom. (The Greek word was *Gehenna*, and the Hebrew word was *ge Hinnom*.)

Gehenna

In the New Testament, the word *Gehenna*, meaning "hell" is used eleven times by Jesus:

> "Do not be afraid of those who kill the body but cannot kill the soul. Rather, be afraid of the One who can destroy both soul and body in hell (*Gehenna*)."
> *Matthew 10:28*

What are the gifts of the Holy Spirit?

Gifts

Gifts of the Holy Spirit are often called "spiritual" or "charismatic" gifts, from the Greek word *charismata*. They are given by the Holy Spirit mainly for the service of fellow Christians.

Five lists of gifts

In the New Testament there are five places where the gifts of the Holy Spirit are mentioned.

Romans 12:6-8
- Prophesying.
- Serving.
- Teaching.
- Encouraging.
- Giving money.
- Leadership.
- Being merciful.

"We have different gifts, according to the grace given to us. If a man's gift is prophesying, let him use it in proportion to his faith. If it is serving, let him serve; if it is teaching, let him teach; if it is encouraging, let him encourage; if it is contributing to the needs of others, let him give generously; if it is leadership, let him govern diligently; if it is showing mercy, let him do it cheerfully."
Romans 12:6-8

1 Corinthians 12:4-11
- Wisdom.
- Knowledge.
- Faith.
- Healing.
- Power to perform miracles.
- Prophecy.
- Distinguishing between spirits.
- Speaking in tongues.
- Interpretation of tongues.

"There are different kinds of gifts, but the same Spirit. There are different kinds of service, but the same Lord. There are different kinds of working, but the same God works all of them in all men.

Now to each one the manifestation of the Spirit is given for the common good. To one there is given through the Spirit the message of wisdom, to another the message of knowledge by means of the same Spirit, to another faith by the same Spirit, to another gifts of healing by that one Spirit, to another miraculous powers, to another prophecy, to another distinguishing between spirits, to another speaking in different kinds of tongues, and to still another the interpretation of tongues.

All these are the work of one and the same Spirit, and he gives them to each one, just as he determines."
1 Corinthians 12:4-11

1 Corinthians 12:28-30
• Apostles.
• Prophets.
• Teachers.
• Miracle workers.
• Healers.
• Helpers.
• Administrators.
• Speakers in tongues.

"And in the Church God has appointed first of all apostles, second prophets, third teachers, then workers of miracles, also those having gifts of healing, those able to help others, those with gifts of administration, and those speaking in different kinds of tongues. Are all apostles? Are all prophets? Are all teachers? Do all work miracles? Do all have gifts of healing? Do all speak in tongues? Do all interpret? But eagerly desire the greater gifts."
1 Corinthians 12:28-30

Ephesians 4:7-8, 11-13
• Apostles.
• Prophets.
•.Evangelists.
• Pastors and teachers.

"But to each one of us grace has been given as Christ apportioned it. This is why it says:
'When he ascended on high, he led captives in his train and gave gifts to men.'"
Ephesians 4:7-8

"It was he who gave some to be apostles, some to be prophets, some to be evangelists, and some to be pastors and teachers, to prepare God's people for works of service, so that the body of Christ may be built up until we all reach unity in the faith and in the knowledge of the Son of God and become mature, attaining to the whole measure of the fulness of Christ." *Ephesians 4:11-13*

1 Peter 4:10-11
• Speaking.
• Serving.

"Each one should use whatever gift he has received to serve others, faithfully administering God's grace in its various forms. If anyone speaks, he should do it as one speaking the very words of God. If anyone serves, he should do it with the strength God provides, so that in all things God may be praised through Jesus Christ." *1 Peter 4:10-11*

Is it necessary to believe in the virgin birth?

Mary's pregnancy

"This is how the birth of Jesus Christ came about: his mother Mary was pledged to be married to Joseph, but before they came together, she was found to be with child through the Holy Spirit."
Matthew 1:18

"Pledged to be married" was a more binding relationship than our present-day engagement. It could only be ended by a divorce. The Jews did not have sexual intercourse during this time of betrothal.

Mary's pregnancy was not the result of any human action, but was due to the direct intervention of the Holy Spirit.

Joseph is helped in his understanding

"Because Joseph her husband was a righteous man and did not want to expose her to public disgrace, he had in mind to divorce her quietly.

But after he had considered this, an angel of the Lord appeared to him in a dream and said, 'Joseph son of David, do not be afraid to take Mary home as your wife, because what is conceived in her is from the Holy Spirit.'" *Matthew 1:19-20*

This is a good summary of the divine conception of Jesus. To be completely accurate, we should refer to the "virgin conception" of Jesus, rather than the "virgin birth" of Jesus.

The Virgin Birth is important

The virgin birth is fundamental to the Christian faith. In order for the sacrifice of Jesus to save the world, Jesus had to be both God and human. If he had been only a man, he would have been just another sinner who had inherited Adam's tendency to sin. If he had been only God, he would not have been an appropriate sacrifice. As both God and man, he was the perfect sacrifice.

Fulfilled prophecy

"All this took place to fulfill what the Lord had said through the prophet: 'The virgin will be with child and will give birth to a son, and they will call him Immanuel.'" *Matthew 1:22-23, quoting Isaiah 7:14*

Mary was a virgin

The angel Gabriel told Mary, "You will be with child and give birth to a son." *Luke 1:31*

Mary asked the angel, "How can this be, since I am a virgin?" *Luke 1:34*

Gabriel replied, "The Holy Spirit will come upon you, and the power of the Most High will overshadow you." *Luke 1:35*

People doubt Jesus' miraculous birth

In his own lifetime, people expressed their doubts about Jesus' miraculous conception. In his home town of Nazareth people asked, "Isn't this the carpenter's son?" *Matthew 13:55*

The Jews deliberately spoke about Jesus' birth as if it were just a normal one: "At this time the Jews began to grumble about [Jesus] because he said, 'I am the bread that came down from heaven.' They said, 'Is this not Jesus, the son of Joseph, whose father and mother we know?'" *John 6:41-42*

Why doesn't the word "Trinity" appear in the Bible?

Trinity

The word *Trinitas* was first used by Tertullian in about A.D. 190. It became part of the "official" teaching of the Christian Church at the Council of Nicea in A.D. 325.

The word "Trinity" means "tri-unity" or "three-in-one." The word is applied to God as he reveals himself in three distinct and inseparable ways in the Bible.

Theologians

Christian theologians formulated the doctrine of the Trinity to counter heretical teaching. While the actual word "Trinity" does not appear, the Bible does contain what the early Christian teachers sought to say about God the Father, God the Son, and God the Holy Spirit.

- There is only one God.
- The Father, the Son, and the Holy Spirit are all God.
- The Father, the Son, and the Holy Spirit are distinct from each other.

The Trinity at work in the Bible

Each member of the Trinity has special spheres of activity.

Member of the Trinity	Sphere of activity	Bible reference
God the Father	Creation	"In the beginning God created the heavens and the earth." *Genesis 1:1*
God the Son	Redemption	"But when the time had fully come, God sent his Son, ... to redeem those under the law." *Galatians 4:5*
God the Spirit	To live in believers	"And if the Spirit of him who raised Jesus from the dead is living in you, he who raised Christ from the dead will also give life to your mortal bodies through his Spirit, who lives in you." *Romans 8:11*

Jobshare

There is a great deal of overlapping in what each member of the Trinity does.

Creation

• The Son was present at creation: "In the beginning was the Word [i.e. Jesus]. ... He was with God in the beginning... Through him all things were made; without him nothing was made that has been made." *John 1:1-4*

• The Spirit was active in creation: "The Spirit of God was hovering over the waters." *Genesis 1:2*

Redemption

• The Father "sent" the Son to redeem us, *see Galatians 4:4*

• God the Father so loved the world that he "sent" his only Son, *see John 3:16.*

Living in believers

• Jesus is said to live in Christians "so that Christ may dwell in your hearts through faith." *Ephesians 3:17*

Father, Son, and Holy Spirit linked in scripture

• "Jesus answered: ... 'I will ask the Father, and he will give you another Counsellor to be with you for ever – the Spirit of truth.'" *John 14:9, 16-17*

• "Jesus said, ... 'Therefore go and make disciples of all nations, baptizing them in the name of the Father and of the Son and of the Holy Spirit.'" *Matthew 28:18-19*

• "May the grace of the Lord Jesus Christ, and the love of God, and the fellowship of the Holy Spirit be with you all." *2 Corinthians 13:14*

Jesus' baptism

The Father, the Son, and the Spirit are clearly seen working together during Jesus' baptism.

• The Father speaks, the "voice from heaven.'

• The Son is baptized.

• The Spirit of God descends.

"As soon as Jesus was baptized, he went up out of the water. At that moment heaven was opened, and he saw the Spirit of God descending like a dove and lighting on him. And a voice from heaven said, 'This is my Son, whom I love; with whom I am well pleased.'" *Matthew 3:16-17*

This unique unity has been compared to water (H_2O). It appears in three forms: as liquid, as solid ice, and as steam – yet is all the same substance.

Why did Jesus die?

Because he was taken by surprise? No!

Jesus repeatedly predicted his own death. He said:

- Where it would happen.
- Who would be instrumental in putting him to death.
- The kind of death he would suffer.
- That he would rise from the dead.

"From that time on Jesus began to explain to his disciples that he must go to Jerusalem and suffer many things at the hands of the elders, chief priests and teachers of the law, and that he must be killed and on the third day be raised to life." *Matthew 16:21*

Because he was powerless to resist? No!

This is certainly what Pilate thought. "Don't you realize I have power either to free you or to crucify you?" *John 19:10*

Jesus answered Pilate, "You would have no power over me if it were not given to you from above." *John 19:11*

The reasons Jesus died

• To show how much God loves us
"But God demonstrates his own love for us in this. While we were still sinners Christ died for us." *Romans 5:8*

• To be our mediator
"For there is one God and one mediator between God and men, the man Christ Jesus, who gave himself as a ransom for all men." *1 Timothy 2:5-6*

• To deal with our sins
"He himself bore our sins in his body on the tree ... by his wounds you have been healed." *1 Peter 2:24*
"God made [Jesus] to be sin for us." *2 Corinthians 5:21*

• To reconcile us to God
"God was reconciling the world to himself in Christ." *2 Corinthians 5:19*

Because he wanted to be a martyr? No!

Jesus' death was much more than the death of a martyr. A martyr suffers physically for a cause or person. Jesus suffered spiritually as well as physically when he died.

Let's contrast the experience of Stephen the martyr with Jesus, who was more than a martyr.

Stephen had a sense of serenity and peace	Jesus did not die serenely or peacefully: "He began to be deeply distressed and troubled. 'My soul is overwhelmed with sorrow to the point of death,' he said to them." *Mark 14:33-34*
Stephen had no desire to escape	Jesus asked if there was a way out for him: "Abba, Father, everything is possible for you. Take this cup from me." *Mark 14:36*
Stephen had a sense of God's presence	Jesus experienced being abandoned by God: "My God, my God, why have you forsaken me?" *Mark 15:34*

What is the way to salvation?

The bridge
Jesus is the bridge for us from death to life.

Everyone has sinned
• "All have sinned and fall short of the glory of God.' *Romans 3:23*
• "We all, like sheep, have gone astray, each of us has turned to his own way.' *Isaiah 53:6*

The penalty sin brings: spiritual death
• "The wages of sin is death, but the gift of God is eternal life in Christ Jesus our Lord." *Romans 6:23*
• "Just as man is destined to die once, and after that to face judgment." *Hebrews 9:27*

Salvation cannot be gained by good deeds
• "For it is by grace you have been saved, through faith – and this is not from yourselves, it is the gift of God – not by works, so that no one can boast." *Ephesians 2:8-9*
• "He saved us, not because of righteous things we had done, but because of his mercy." *Titus 3:5*

The cross of Jesus

Jesus pays the penalty for our sins by dying on the cross.

- "But God demonstrates his own love for us in this: while we were still sinners, Christ died for us." *Romans 5:8*
- "For Christ died for sins once for all, the righteous for the unrighteous, to bring you to God." *1 Peter 3:18*

Jesus must be welcomed and received

- "Yet to all who received him, to those who believed in his name, he gave the right to become children of God." *John 1:12*
- "Here I am! I stand at the door and knock. If anyone hears my voice and opens the door, I will come in and eat with him, and he with me." *Revelation 3:20*

The steps to salvation

- We have to admit that we are sinners. *See Romans 3:23*
- We have to believe that Jesus died for our sins. *See 1 Peter 3:18*
- We have to confess our sins to God and wish to turn from them. *See 1 John 1:9*
- We must willingly accept God's gracious free gift of salvation and then turn our lives over to Jesus Christ. *See Ephesians 2:8-9; Titus 3:4-7; Acts 16:31-33*

See also: *How can I know for sure that I belong to Jesus?*, page 54.

What does the Bible say about being born again?

Born-again Christians

People sometimes talk about "born-again Christians," as if there are two types of Christian – those who have been born again and those who have not. According to the Bible, there is only one kind of Christian. We either "have" Jesus or we do not.

> "He who has the Son has life; he who does not have the Son of God does not have life."
> *1 John 5:12*
> "… if anyone does not have the Spirit of Christ, he does not belong to Christ." *Romans 8:9b*

One way of describing a Christian is to say that he or she has been born again.

Nicodemus

The expression "born again" is used by Jesus in his conversation with a top-ranking Jewish leader, Nicodemus. Jesus explains to Nicodemus that becoming a true follower is such a big turn-around, it is like being born again.

> "Jesus declared, 'I tell you the truth, no one can see the kingdom of God unless he is born again.'
> 'How can a man be born when he is old?' Nicodemus asked. 'Surely he cannot enter a second time into his mother's womb to be born!'
> Jesus answered, 'I tell you the truth, no one can enter the kingdom of God unless he is born of water and the Spirit. Flesh gives birth to flesh, but the Spirit gives birth to spirit. You should not be surprised at my saying, "You must be born again."'" *John 3:3-7*

Names used to describe Jesus' followers

Name	Used by	Bible reference
Follower	Jesus	Jesus said to Matthew, "Follow me." *Matthew 9:9*
Christian	People in Antioch	"The disciples were called Christians first at Antioch." *Acts 11:26*
Servant	Paul	"Paul, a servant of Christ Jesus." *Romans 1:1*
Nazarenes	Tertullus	"He is a ringleader of the Nazarene sect." *Acts 24:5*
Brothers	Jesus	"Pointing to his disciples, [Jesus] said, 'Here are my mother and my brothers.' " *Matthew 12:49*
Disciples	Jesus	"Anyone who does not carry his cross and follow me cannot be my disciple." *Luke 14:27*
Friends	Jesus	"I have called you friends." *John 15:15*
Soldier	Paul	"Like a good soldier of Christ Jesus." *2 Timothy 2:3*
Saints	John	"For the righteous acts of the saints." *Revelation 19:8*

Words linked to "born again"

• New birth.	"He has given us new birth." *1 Peter 1:3*
• New creation.	"If anyone is in Christ, he is a new creation; the old has gone, the new has come!" *2 Corinthians 5:17*
• God gives birth.	"You deserted the Rock, who fathered you; you forgot the God who gave you birth." *Deuteronomy 32:18*
• Born of God.	"Everyone who loves has been born of God and knows God." *1 John 4:7*
• Child of God	"To all who received him, to those who believed in his name, he gave the right to become children of God." *John 1:12*

Why get baptized?

The meaning of the word

The Greek verb for "to baptize" is *baptizo*, meaning "to dip" or "to immerse."

- John the Baptist challenged people to be baptized by him in the River Jordan. Being immersed in water symbolized having sin washed away. "Confessing their sins, they were baptized by [John] in the Jordan River." *Matthew 3:6*
- Jesus was baptized "to fulfill all righteousness." *Matthew 3:15*

Links to the Holy Spirit

- "When he [the Holy Spirit] comes, he will convict the world of guilt in regard to sin and righteousness and judgment." *John 16:8*
- "Repent and be baptized, every one of you, in the name of Jesus Christ... And you will receive the gift of the Holy Spirit." *Acts 2:38*

Links to the death and resurrection of Jesus

- "Don't you know that all of us who were baptized into Christ Jesus were baptized into his death? We were therefore buried with him through baptism into death in order that, just as Christ was raised from the dead through the glory of the Father, we too may live a new life." *Romans 6:3-4*

Baptism and conversion

In the New Testament, as soon as people put their trust in Jesus, they were baptized as a sign of their new-found faith.

• 3,000 people

"Peter said, "Repent and be baptized, everyone of you, in the name of Jesus Christ for the forgiveness of your sins.'"... Those who accepted his message were baptized, and about three thousand were added to their number that day." *Acts 2:38, 41*

• The Ethiopian official

"Philip ... told him the good news about Jesus. As they traveled along the road, they came to some water and the eunuch said, "Look, here is water. Why shouldn't I be baptized?" And he gave orders to stop the chariot. Then both Philip and the eunuch went down into the water and Philip baptized him." *Acts 8:35-38*

• Saul [Paul]

"Ananias ... placing his hands on Saul, ... said, "Brother Saul, the Lord – Jesus, who appeared to you on the road as you were coming here – has sent me so that you may see again and be filled with the Holy Spirit." Immediately, something like scales fell from Saul's eyes, and he could see again. He got up and was baptized." *Acts 9:17-18*

Babies and baptism

The New Testament does not give any directions on whether or not babies should be baptized. One argument put forward in favor of baptism is that in Old Testament times, baby boys were circumcised when they were eight days old, as a sign of God's blessing and inclusion in God's family (see Genesis 17:10-11). There are a few examples of whole households, adults and possibly children, being baptized in the New Testament: "I also baptized the household of Stephanus." *1 Corinthians 1:16*

The jailor at Philippi believed in Jesus at midnight, "and all his family were baptized." *Acts 16:33*

Jesus said Christians were to baptize

Almost the last recorded words of Jesus in Matthew's Gospel are, "Therefore go and make disciples of all nations, baptizing them in the name of the Father and of the Son and of the Holy Spirit." *Matthew 28:19*

What's the point of the Lord's Supper?

Old Testament background

The Passover was celebrated in Old Testament times, and once a year in the Temple in Jesus' day, to remember God's deliverance of his people from slavery in Egypt. The story is told in the Book of Exodus.

• Kill a lamb

"Each man is to take a lamb for his family ... All the people ... must slaughter them at twilight. Then they are to take some of the blood and put it on the sides and tops of the door-frames of the houses where they eat the lambs. That same night they are to eat the meat roasted over the fire, along with bitter herbs, and bread made without yeast." *Exodus 12:3, 6-8*

• "I will pass over you"

"... On that same night I will pass through Egypt and strike down every firstborn – both men and animals – and I will bring judgment on all the gods of Egypt. I am the LORD. The blood will be a sign for you on the houses where you are; and when I see the blood, I will pass over you. No destructive plague will touch you when I strike Egypt." *Exodus 12:12-13*

The Passover and the Lord's Supper

Jesus linked the eating of the Passover meal with his disciples to his own suffering.

"He said to them, 'I have eagerly desired to eat this Passover with you before I suffer.'" *Luke 22:15*

The first Lord's Supper was when Jesus transformed the Passover. Matthew tells us exactly what happened:

"While they were eating, Jesus took bread, gave thanks and broke it, and gave it to his disciples, saying, 'Take and eat; this is my body.' Then he took the cup, gave thanks and offered it to them, saying, 'Drink from it, all of you. This is my blood of the covenant, which is poured out for many for the forgiveness of sins.'" *Matthew 26:26-28*

Jesus as the sacrificial lamb

There are many obvious symbols surrounding the Lord's Supper which were clearly not lost on his followers.

The lamb

• "Christ, our Passover lamb," writes Paul. *1 Corinthians 5:7*
• John the Baptist, on seeing Jesus: "Look, the Lamb of God, who takes away the sin of the world!" *John 1:29*
• Peter writes about "the precious blood of Christ." He says that Jesus was the perfect sacrificial lamb, "a lamb without blemish or defect." *1 Peter 1:19*

The bread and wine

Jesus broke the bread and handed around a cup of wine. This symbolized his own body, which would also shortly be broken, and his own blood, which would soon be shed.

Different names

In the contemporary Christian Church, the Lord's Supper is called a variety of different names.
• **The Lord's Supper.**
• **Holy Communion.**
• **Agape.**
• **Fellowship meal.**
• **Love feast.**
• **Eucharist (thanksgiving).**
• **Breaking of bread.**

Why do we have Lord's Supper services today?

Jesus said, "Do this in remembrance of me." *Luke 22:19*

The first Christians usually came together on the first day of the week to break bread. *See Acts 20:7.*

"They broke bread in their homes and ate together with glad and sincere hearts." *Acts 2:46*

Paul warned the Christians at Corinth not to take part in the Lord's Supper in an unworthy manner:

"A man ought to examine himself before he eats of the bread and drinks of the cup. For anyone who eats and drinks without recognizing the body of the Lord eats and drinks judgment on himself." *1 Corinthians 11:28-29*

Will Christians face persecution?

Jesus warned his followers to expect persecution

Jesus never tried to hide the fact that his followers would be constantly under fire.

"They will lay hands on you and persecute you. They will deliver you to synagogues and prisons, and you will be brought before kings and governors, and all on account of my name." *Luke 21:12*

New Testament martyrs

John the Baptist
John the Baptist was beheaded because he told Herod that he should not be living with Herodias, his brother Philip's wife. "The king ... had John beheaded in the prison." *Matthew 14:9-10*

Stephen
"They all rushed at him, dragged him out of the city and began to stone him. Meanwhile, the witnesses laid their clothes at the feet of a young man named Saul.

While they were stoning him, Stephen prayed, 'Lord Jesus, receive my spirit.' Then he fell on his knees and cried out, 'Lord, do not hold this sin against them.' When he had said this, he fell asleep.

And Saul was there, giving approval to his death." *Acts 7:57–8:1*

James
James' martyrdom is the only record in the Bible of the death of an apostle. We are told that King Herod began to persecute some members of the Church: "He had James, the brother of John, put to death by the sword." *Acts 12:2.* However, there are accounts, of varying reliability, which point to Andrew, Peter, James the brother of Jesus, and Paul being martyred.

Jesus told James and John, "You will drink of the same cup [of suffering] that I drink." *Mark 10:9*

Persecution of the early Christians

The Acts of the Apostles records how the first Christians were persecuted and hounded from one city to another.

Peter and John put in jail

"They were greatly disturbed because the apostles were teaching the people and proclaiming in Jesus the resurrection of the dead. They seized Peter and John, and because it was evening, they put them in jail." *Acts 4:2-3*

Apostles arrested

"Then the high priest and all his associates, who were members of the party of the Sadducees, were filled with jealousy. They arrested the apostles and put them in the public jail. But during the night an angel of the Lord opened the doors of the jail and brought them out." *Acts 5:17-19*

Apostles flogged

"They called the apostles in and had them flogged." *Acts 5:40*

Christians scattered by persecution

"Now those who had been scattered by the persecution in connection with Stephen traveled as far as Phoenicia, Cyprus and Antioch." *Acts 11:19*

Herod puts Peter in prison

"It was about this time that King Herod arrested some who belonged to the Church, intending to persecute them. ... He proceeded to seize Peter. ... After arresting him, he put him in prison." *Acts 12:1, 3-4*

Paul's summary

Paul, perhaps more than any of the other apostles, knew for himself what it meant to suffer persecution for Jesus: "In fact, everyone who wants to live a godly life in Christ Jesus will be persecuted." *2 Timothy 3:12*

Statistics tell us that in the twentieth century, more Christian believers have been killed for their faith than in all the previous nineteen centuries combined.

How can I know for sure that I belong to Jesus?

Certainty

A Chinese Christian was once asked how he could be certain that Jesus had come into his life. He replied, "Jesus has said it. He is God. He cannot lie. I trust him."

- Jesus said, "I tell you the truth, whoever hears my words and believes him who sent me has eternal life and will not be condemned; he has crossed over from death to life." *John 5:24*
- Paul said, "There is now no condemnation for those who are in Christ Jesus." *Romans 8:1*

John's Gospel

John tells us that he wrote his gospel so that we would believe in Jesus.

- "Jesus did many other miraculous signs in the presence of his disciples, which are not recorded in this book. But these are written that you may believe that Jesus is the Christ, the Son of God, and that by believing you may have life in his name." *John 20:30-31*

Firm foundations

John wants new Christians to have a firm hold on their faith in Jesus. He sets out the things that Christians can be certain about.

Obedience

- Obey his commands:
"We know that we have come to know [Jesus] if we obey his commands." *1 John 2:3*
- Obey his word:
"But if anyone obeys his word, God's love is truly made complete in him." *1 John 2:5*

The Holy Spirit

- Christians are anointed by God's Spirit:
"You have an anointing from the Holy One, and all of you *know* the truth." *1 John 2:20*
- We know by the Spirit:
"And this is how we *know* that he lives in us. We know it by the Spirit he gave us." *1 John 3:24*
- The Spirit is God's gift:
"We *know* that we live in him and he in us, because he has given us of his Spirit." *1 John 4:13*

Love for fellow Christians

- "We *know* that we have passed from death to life, because we love our brothers." *1 John 3:14*
- "This is how we *know* who the children of God are and who the children of the Devil are: anyone who does not do what is right is not a child of God; nor is anyone who does not love his brother." *1 John 3:10-11*

A sense of God's presence

- "This then is how we *know* that we belong to the truth, and how we set our hearts at rest in his presence whenever our hearts condemn us." *1 John 3:19-20*

Acknowledgement of Jesus

- "If anyone acknowledges that Jesus is the Son of God, God lives in him and he in God. And so we *know* and rely on the love God has for us." *1 John 4:15-16*

The First Letter of John

John also clearly states why he wrote his first letter. It was a letter to believers in Jesus, to help them know for certain that they belonged to Jesus:

- "I write these things to you who believe in the name of the Son of God so that you may know that you have eternal life." *1 John 5:13*

What do I need to do to grow as a Christian?

Abide in Jesus

"Remain in me, and I will remain in you. No branch can bear fruit by itself; it must remain in the vine. Neither can you bear fruit unless you remain in me.

I am the vine; you are the branches. If a man remains in me and I in him, he will bear much fruit; apart from me you can do nothing.

If anyone does not remain in me, he is like a branch that is thrown away and withers; such branches are picked up, thrown into the fire and burned. If you remain in me and my words remain in you, ask whatever you wish, and it will be given you. This is to my Father's glory, that you bear much fruit, showing yourselves to be my disciples." *John 15:4-8*

The results of abiding in Jesus

Spiritual growth
"If a man remain in me and I in him, he will bear much fruit." *John 15:5*

Answered prayer
"If you remain in me and my words remain in you, ask whatever you wish, and it will be given you." *John 15:7*

A new life
"Therefore, if anyone is in Christ, he is a new creation, the old has gone, the new has come!" *2 Corinthians 5:17*

Peace
"I have told you these things, so that in me you may have peace." *John 16:33*

Working for God
"For we are God's workmanship, created in Christ Jesus to do good works, which God prepared in advance for us to do." *Ephesians 2:10*